Copyright © 2025 by Gary T. Rodgers Jr.

For permissions or inquiries, contact:
grodgers064@gmail.com

First Edition, 2025

I have so many memories of my father and his music downloaded in my mind it seems like I can just think back and they start to play out like scenes from a movie. I can recall sitting and staring at the black- and-white pictures of his band that were on our living room wall. They had some of the coldest poses and their style was always a magnificent display of showmanship. Every photo blended an authentic coolness with impeccable taste for fashion. They remind me of the O'Jays. Our house at 3621 Regatta Way in the west end of Louisville, Kentucky served as a practice space for my dad and his friends, Robert Ford and William (Billy or Brad) Bradley (McPhatter).

After they finished their shifts at G&G Auto Cleaners they came here to work.

I still hear my mom saying something like.
"Here they come, y'all! It's time to go!"
I always loved being around the music, so
they let me play on the piano, the guitars,
beat on the drums and even sing on the
microphones. Those were great times and
as they say "History in the Making."

My mom tried to make sure that we stayed out of the way during rehearsal time. We had band members always coming to our house, or Daddy was going out working on some music business. Whenever someone arrived with their instruments, I was always ready to help them carry everything inside. I was really helping set up the stage, and before long, everyone would be jamming. First Robert, Billy, and then my Daddy would come in and they step to the mic one, two, then fingers snap in synch to the beat. The right hand goes up, then down, then Rob, Brad, and Gary spin, then bang! Brad goes into falsetto, and they start to do their thing on the three mic stands posted in the center.

I always knew it was only a matter of time before Daddy or someone else would say, "Okay, Lil Rodge, let's go, buddy. We've got work to do." That was my cue to go to bed or at least get out of their way. It was always disappointing to be sent away from a free concert, but it didn't matter, because the music would still be pumping all through the house. I was always happy, feeling comfy and cozy, but never wanting to fall asleep on so many nights. Sometimes I would wake up with one leg in and one leg out of my bed. Many memories of those songs and all of those tunes still stick in my head today.

How can anyone sleep with a crash of the cymbals and the beat of the drums pumping through the house and the singing live full blast in the next room.

I remember one new guy who came by to audition or try out for the group. My sister and I agreed we didn't like the man and didn't want him in (our) group because we only liked Billy, and Robert.

We came up with a plan when he goes to the restroom we set him up to trip him with a broom we were playing with in the hallway. The only thing about the plan is, It worked. The guy actually tripped and fell down in the hallway. He was ok. lol. but this stuff is too hilarious, just funny remembering things from when we were little. I tried to stay close by or in the mix at all times possible. I couldn't help the urge of peeping out my door to see what was going on in the living room. I was watching and wanting to be like them.

One day, I went with my Dad, we took a ride, and pulled up to "Big A Shopping Center." It was a poppin' strip mall in Louisville at the time. We entered a Record Store where the logo on the door said "Stick it in Your Ear." Once we went inside, I immediately smelled the fragrance of incense and heard music playing.

We went into this back room that had those stringed beads hanging down from the doorway, and a few minutes later, a man walked in and shook hands with my Dad. My Dad turned to me and said Gary, this is Bobby Lester and we shook hands. Once we got back home, sitting on the couch, Daddy pulled out an album with a big Moon with a face on it.

He put it on the record player and we started listening. We listened to this record over and over again, and every day, Daddy would listen to this record, which was the Moonglows. He explained that the Moonglows were Doo Wop Legends and he's about to start working with Bobby Lester.

Bobby is one of the guys who started the Original Moonglows and now he's going to be one of them.

Before we knew it, Daddy was going on long road trips. Every time he had to leave, Rikita would jump on his legs and hold on tight, she didn't want to let him go. Mama would always be sad, though she played it off pretty well. Years later, by the time I was a teenager around '83, we were just seeing Dad every once in a while as he was on the road. He had some people running the shop by then but that's a story for another time.

He'd call home to check in, and we'd all get a chance to talk. I'd hear, "Garyeee! Come to the phone!" and I'd come running, waiting for my turn to talk. I'd always ask, Daddy, Where are you now?" He'd say something like, "Corpus Christi, Texas," or Montreal, Canada, and start telling me about all the places they were going.

It was all cool to hear, but for real, I was missing him a lot.

What none of us realized at the time was just how deep this became. He was into something big. He was rehearsing even more intently, tightening up those harmonies, running the old Moonglows' music like it was brand new. Every detail of the show mattered; he was locked in. Night after night, they'd run through those classic arrangements until it felt like magic in motion. The group was quickly getting reestablished, especially with Bobby Lester back and in great form full of excitement for taking on this new venture.

His voice still had that unmistakable smoothness, that effortless glide that had once defined a generation of sound. With Gary by his side, they became like real Brothers, focused, driven, almost obsessive about getting every harmony right. It felt like lightning striking twice for Bobby.

That connection between them reignited something powerful. It wasn't just about reviving old hits; it was about restoring a legacy, breathing life back into something sacred. The difference between this comeback and others was. The Moonglows weren't just a nostalgic act; they were stepping back into the spotlight with purpose. They weren't performing for applause; they were performing to reclaim their rightful place in the story of American music. The Doo-Wop era might've faded from the mainstream, but what they were doing out there on those stages was real. It mattered. They were reminding people where it all started.

As for my Daddy, he wasn't just on the road chasing gigs. He was part of a movement, a living, breathing thing that is music. He was pouring everything he had into making sure it was done right. Long rehearsals, late-night calls, chasing venues, rewriting arrangements, getting the stage presence locked in, he was all in. I can still hear him humming through vocal parts over and over again, bouncing ideas, sometimes sounding tired but always lit up when he talked about the next show.

Looking back, I can see now how much heart and hustle he was putting into it all. At the time, we just wanted him to be home. I know we all did it, my sister Rikita, and especially Mama. All the while, Gary was building on something out there, something bigger than any of us knew existed. Bigger than just one man's career. He was helping rebuild a chapter of Black music history, helping ensure that The Moonglows didn't just fade into the background. He was keeping their sound and their story Alive.

The Moonglows

This is a painting of The Moonglows an American R&B vocal group that didn't ride the wave of musical change; they helped create it.

Born in Louisville, Kentucky, they came onto the scene in the early 1950s with a sound that was smooth, soulful, and undeniably original.

Their signature blend of tight vocal harmonies, tender lyrics, and rich emotional delivery helped define what we now call Doo-Wop, but back then, it was just real music.

It was the soundtrack of real life, record shops, and late-night slow dances across Black America.

The Moonglows

Legend says the group, The Moonglows, was founded around 1952 in Cleveland, Ohio. The story begins with two friends from Louisville, Kentucky. Bobby Lester and Harvey Fuqua. These talented gentlemen shared a love for gospel and harmony singing, then eventually started performing together in church choirs and local talent shows during the late 1940s and early 1950s. Their voices blended naturally, Bobby with his rich, smooth vocals and Harvey with his sharp baritone and dynamic piano skills. Driven by passion and the dream of making it big, they formed a group called "The Crazy Sounds" and moved to Cleveland, Ohio. The Moonglows were ahead of their time, blending jazz, blues, and gospel into a sound that transcended genre boundaries. Together with Prentiss Barnes, Peter Graves, Billy Johnson, Harvey Fuqua, and Bobby Lester, aka The Moonglows, became key players in the early days of Rock and Roll.

Their legacy is a part of history that is not just measured by the number of hits they produced but by their lasting influence on the evolution of Soul and R&B music. They have carved out a place for themselves among the world's most respected vocal groups through persistence, harmony, and innovation.

The Moonglows personified greatness and originality in front of the microphone, on screen, and on stage. Then continued to innovate culture behind the scenes.

The Moonglows

They put out hits like "Sincerely," "Most of All," "See Saw," and "Ten Commandments of Love." The Moonglows weren't just topping charts, they were shaping the future. Their influence would ripple through the decades, touching everyone from The Temptations to Boyz II Men. One of the most notable torch-carriers was Marvin Gaye, who got his true start singing alongside them. It was within the ranks of The Moonglows that Marvin learned to craft harmonies, work stage presence, and other skills that would later power his legendary solo career. Without Harvey and the Moonglows, there might not have been a Marvin Gaye as we know him.

But while history often highlights the frontmen and the biggest names, there were others behind the curtain, like my father, who were every bit as committed to keeping the music alive. By the late 70's, when many thought the doo-wop era had long passed, Daddy was out there helping to bring it back. And not just for nostalgia's sake but for the culture. For the people who still remembered what it meant. This old-school music brought something new to the generations who had never heard it live before. Rehearsals were relentless. Daddy and Bobby Lester locked in, tightening harmonies, reviving old arrangements, and in some cases, reimagining them altogether. It was work, but it was also sacred. There was something spiritual about those sessions about reclaiming the music and making sure it still hit people in the heart. Had Bobby's voice aged? Sure, but it had aged like oak, deeper, wiser, full of soul.

The Moonglows

Never a question about commitment. Gary's desire to Moonglow was unwavering. He wasn't doing this for fame. He was doing it because this music was part of his DNA.

Photo Courtesy UGHA

Alan Freed

[Alan Freed]
(born:1921 – died: 1965)

Alan Freed, was a popular disc jockey at the time who engaged in black music. He became the group's manager and co-writer once he heard them sing for the first time. Freed named the group the Moonglows after his popular Cleveland Moondog Show. They signed with Freed's Champagne label in 1953, they also recorded songs on another small label named Chance, where they recorded a cover of Doris Day's "Secret Love," their most significant release for Chance.

Alan Freed relocated to a New York radio station, WINS. With music friends and industry connections already in place, everything worked well for the Moonglows in Chicago. Their first single from Chess was "Sincerely," led by Lester, which reached number one on the Billboard R&B chart and the top 20 of the pop chart. The song was later a crossover success in a cover version by the McGuire Sisters. Soon, the band picked the guitar player, Billy Johnson, along with Prentiss Barnes and Peter Graves, a cousin of Bobby Lester. That same year, the group had another R&B hit with "Most of All," followed by a favorite of mine, "We Go Together" in 1956. Chess also issued some of their recordings and was credited as the Moonlighters. The Moonglows were a foundational force in the rise of R&B. They were featured in the movie Rock, Rock, Rock with Alan Freed.

Harvey Fuqua

[Harvey Fuqua Jr.]
(born: 1929 - died: 2010)
Harvey Fuqua, Jr. was born in Louisville, KY, the son of Harvey Sr. and Lillian Marshall Fuqua. (Chicago has been mistakenly given as his birth location in some resources.) He was once married to Gwen Gordy, a sister of Berry Gordy (Motown) and is the uncle of Antoine Fuqua Film Director of Training Day.

Fuqua had an extensive career as a singer, songwriter, record producer, talent scout, developer, and manager. He owned Tri-Phi Records and Harvey Records also helped develop Motown Records in Detroit, MI. He co-founded the Moonglows, a doo-wop group, with Bobby Lester (from Louisville), Alexander Graves, and Prentiss Barnes; he sometimes shared the lead vocals with Lester. Fuqua and Lester sung together in high school, and Fuqua also sang with Barnes in Cleveland when they were members of Crazy Sounds, this union would become the Moonglows.

In Detroit, the Moonglows Harvey Fuqua gave Marvin Gaye his start, and Fuqua helped produce the song " Sexual Healing " plus a number of other songs by other artists. The Moonglows were inducted into the Rock and Roll Hall of Fame in 2000.

Bobby Lester

[Bobby Lester Robert L. Dallas]
(born: 1930 - died: 1980)

Bobby Lester, was a tenor singer, he was born in Louisville, Kentucky to Alberta Dallas. Bobby Lester's voice, smooth like velvet and he wrote beautiful songs. Many of those with Harvey Fuqua playing piano when both were teens, first performing around 1949.

They later became the first members of the Moonglows group in Cleveland, Ohio. Lester was the lead singer on most of the group's recordings from 1952-1960.

Before the group became a hit, Lester worked in a coal yard by day and sang at night. One of the group's best known accolades is for their biggest hit entitled " Sincerely ," released in December 1954. It was said that Frank Sinatra Claimed "Bobby Lester had the best voice he has ever heard."

With success also came major changes as the core members split. The group became known as Bobby Lester and the Moonglows for a brief period.

The Moonglows

Around 1960, Bobby Lester returned to Louisville as Harvey
continued in success in his solo realm.
Bobby was managing a nightclub in 1970 when he revived the New
Moonglows.
The New Moonglows lasted for a couple of years and then
reformed again in 1972 with Lester, Fuqua, Alexander Graves,
Chuck Lewis, and Doc Williams.
They recorded an album entitled The Return of the Moonglows.
The group broke apart and then was restructured again
in 1978. Bobby Lester continued as a leader until he passed away
in Louisville, the year was 1980.

After Bobby's death, his Moonglows continued performing per
Bobby's blessing with the new leader Gary Rodgers.
The Moonglows were inducted into the Rock and Roll Hall of
Fame in the year 2000.

Gary Rodgers

[Gary Thomas Rodgers]
(born: April 3, 1951 -died: June 25, 2005)

Gary Rodgers grew up in the West End of Louisville, Kentucky. He was born to Henrietta and Edward Rodgers. His mom played the piano. Some of his early interest came in the form of Doo-Wop harmonies like the soulful crooners spinning on his parents' record player. From a young age, Gary had a voice that stopped people in their tracks, smooth, clear, and powerful. He had big plans after graduating. He desired to go on to Seminary school to become a priest in the Catholic Faith. While he attended Flaget High School, Gary wasn't just known for his voice, he was also a star football player. At a glance, he was super-fast, and strong for a running back. These assets paid off for Flaget as the games were packed to see the Rodgers Run, he was one of the most sought after football players in the country. Gary was tough and earned his respect across the city and statewide. But no matter how much he shined and showed out on the field, the stage, and the microphone, called to him the loudest.

His teammates said that Gary would be very quiet before games and kept all to himself. After he got his work done on the field and after securing the win, Gary came back on the bus ride roaring like a lion, just fired up. While in his teenage years, Gary dabbled around singing with friends in the neighborhood.

A few years later, Gary met a girl named Shawn Dulin. She attended Shawnee High School. Although Gary was working, playing sports, and attending school, the two grew close. In 1970, they welcomed their first child, Gary Jr.

The following year, they were married and celebrated the birth of their second child, a daughter, Rikita. Balancing a new family, a growing music career, and a hands-on car detail shop, Gary still set his sights on discovering his dreams for the music world. By day, he ran his detail business and began generating income to support his young family. Gary, alongside his wife Shawn, was a young couple with the life of a storybook. By night, the group was performing and playing various gigs around the city. This was everyday life, working and rehearsing with his group, taking care of family, occasional fishing trips and chasing musical dreams. Gary, Robert Ford, and William Bradley, son of legendary Clyde McPhatter, formed a group and made music magic.

I remember them rehearsing in our living room, the furniture pushed to the sides, the coffee table moved out of the way, and the air thick with concentration and harmony. The room would fill with sound. Smooth, layered vocals that danced off the walls and seemed to bring the very soul of the house alive. It wasn't flashy or high-tech, just voices, heart, and purpose. That living room became their music proving ground, their sanctuary, their first stage.

For Gary, music wasn't just something he loved it was a lifeline. It gave him focus, direction, and an outlet for expression that went deeper than words. In those quiet hours of the night, when most people were winding down, Gary came to life refining vocal runs, experimenting with transitions, obsessing over tone and timing. His vision was clear and his mind was sharp. He wasn't in it for applause; he was in it for excellence. During those late-night rehearsals, Gary, Robert, and "Brad" began to make things shift. It wasn't just fun anymore it was intentional.

They made a decision right there in that living room that they weren't going to be just another vocal group. They were the best that ever did this. That wasn't a boast; it was a vow to each other, and to the music. They knew they had something rare: a blend of voices that really sounded like money, a natural chemistry that didn't need to be forced, and all backed up with mutual hunger to chase greatness. Their connection was more than musical it was personal. They trusted each other. They pushed each other. When one missed a note, the others were right there to help tighten it up. When the groove hit just right, they knew it without saying a word. It was a kind of harmony that went beyond the music a brotherhood forged in hard work, laughter, and an unspoken understanding of what they were building.

That foundation laid right there in the living room would go on to power one of Louisville's most exciting and talked-about vocal acts to this day. They brought the spirit of those nights into every performance: raw talent shaped by relentless practice, anchored in respect for the legends before them but propelled by their own bold ambition. From those humble rehearsals, they created something unforgettable. And it all started with three voices, a living room, and the belief that they could and would be great.

Mastering The Harmonies

As Gary's reputation grew, he continued to work and organize the band, also continuing rehearsals with Robert Ford and Bill Bradley. Their practice sessions had full bands set up, and they jammed for hours, stepping routines in our living room, on the front porch steps, and outside under streetlights they had the glow guiding their dreams and sharpening their sound. It wasn't long before word reached the owner of a small but bustling club on Oak Street known for showcasing local talent in Louisville. One humid summer evening, the trio was invited to open the show.

They stepped onto the narrow stage in sharp suits with the help of the house band. Performance perfected, outfits clean, ready to throw down. The band tuned right in as the guitars, horns, drums, and their voices made the place go wild.

Their covers of The Platters' and The Drifters' upbeat hits struck a chord. When Gary hit his bass note, the crowd burst into cheers. By the end of the set, the place was buzzing with applause, and the owner offered them a weekly residency slot on the spot. The guys worked and sometimes slept between the gigs at Gary's detail shop. Robert Ford was skilled with a razor blade and was the group's barber many times. Brad was married to a supermodel and singer: Linda Blakely, who later in her career, went on to sing with the Fatback Band. Gary set up the plans for the vision they pitched in and bought tuxedos for their following shows. As they stepped up their performance game, Style of the Gentleman and Sharp suits became their trademark fashion on stage.

Sometimes the guys worked late, really late. Rehearsals would stretch into the early hours, and if they didn't feel like heading home, they'd crash at the Shop. On the floor, slumped on the couch or folding chairs, still humming melodies in their sleep. Other times, they'd end up at our house, filling the kitchen with laughter, low harmony runs, and the smell of whatever Mama had going on the stove. It was fun, it was loud, it was family.

They called their Friday-night gigs "Street-Corner Harmonies."
It was a plug to their roots, those early days when doo-wop groups
would gather under streetlights and on front porches, letting their
voices carry into the night. But now, they were packing out rooms
across Louisville. Small clubs, community centers, anywhere that
would hold a mic and a crowd. People weren't just showing up,
they were following the sound. Folks came in from the West End,
the South End, even from neighboring towns, just to feel that
magic live. It was more than music it was revival.

For Gary, it was never just about the fame . It was the
camaraderie. The bond between him and his two closest
bandmates is tighter than brothers. There was always some
conversation that kept them together for hours. They'd swap
stories, crack jokes, and plot out the future like they were building
an empire. Stepping to original arrangements, adding new songs,
figuring out how to get a tight sound, and even bigger.
Their M/O was always chopping up some "player business."

They knew how to move in the world with confidence and class. It
was strategy, all natural swagger, and soul all in one.

By the end of that summer in 1975, the word was out.
Bookings started rolling in, faster than they could take them all.
Private parties, wedding receptions, club nights, and out-of-town
gigs in places like Lexington, Cincinnati, even Indianapolis.

What started as passion had turned into full motion and what they lacked in big-budget polish, they made up for in heart and hustle. For Gary, music wasn't just something he did. It was who he was. A sound, a style, a way of life that wove itself through every part of his day.

From early morning breakfast sandwiches at the Shop to those midnight harmonies in that same garage. He didn't always say it out loud, but you could see it in the way he carried himself. Always that quiet fire burning, he knew this was only the beginning.

He was building something. And though none of us could see how far it would go yet, we all felt it coming. As the group continued to build momentum, they caught the attention of Louisville music legend Albert "Big Al" Workman.

He had a commanding presence at 6 feet 5 inches and 400 pounds.

Big Al was deeply rooted in the city's music scene through a plethora of talented connects. The Aristocrats Organization and the Influential Mind Liberators were known for leading one of the most dynamic and polished show bands of the 70's era. Big Al's reputation for excellence was unmatched. When he encountered Gary's ensemble, which now featured the striking presence of Louisville-supermodel Linda Blakely, Big Al saw a rare opportunity to reinvent his act. Impressed by their raw talent and unique chemistry, he approached Gary with a proposal to merge their groups under the banner of The Aristocrats Organization. True to his character, Big Al made it clear that the terms would be fair, ensuring Gary's creative leadership and vision would remain central to their collaboration. Gary, always a sharp judge of character, recognized the sincerity in Big Al's offer.

After a few late-night meetings at Big Al's legendary studio on Bardstown Road, where the scent of incense clung to the walls and the sounds of funk, jazz, and gospel bled from every corner, the deal was sealed with a handshake, a nod, and a bottle of aged bourbon. The merger was electric. Rehearsals became showcases of raw talent and unfiltered soul. Linda Blakely, already a star in her own right, brought elegance and high-fashion allure to the group, transforming every performance into an event. Under Big Al's guidance, Gary found himself not just a musician but a leader mentoring younger players, shaping arrangements, and helping define a new, genre-bending sound.

The newly merged act, now officially The Aristocrats Organization, debuted at the historic Seelbach Hotel ballroom. Word spread fast. Industry insiders, local legends, and out-of-town talent scouts packed the venue. That night, under the dimmed chandelier lights and over thunderous applause, a new era of Louisville music was born. Following their explosive debut at the Seelbach, the group now dubbed The Aristocrats, became an unstoppable force in the regional music scene. Their sound was a seamless fusion of classic soul, psychedelic funk, jazz improvisation, and gritty Southern blues, anchored by Gary, Rob and Brad"s sharp arrangements and Big Al's business savvy. Every member had a role, and every performance was a statement.

They began touring the Midwest and Southeast, selling out small theaters, college auditoriums, and underground clubs from Nashville to Indianapolis. Word of mouth spread quickly. Local newspapers ran glowing reviews, calling them "soul of the ville." By the end of that first tour, they had secured a distribution deal with a boutique label out of Chicago that specialized in live performance recordings.

Linda Blakely's star power drew attention from national fashion outlets and lifestyle magazines, who were fascinated by her decision to stay rooted in music rather than transition to Hollywood. Her presence on stage gave the group a unique crossover appeal. Music lovers came for the sound, but left dazzled by the spectacle.

Meanwhile, Big Al and Gary worked behind the scenes to build more than a band; they were building a movement. They organized, opened a small rehearsal studio in West Louisville, and even helped launch a weekend radio program on WLOU. There local talent could be featured on The Aristocrats' latest live recordings. This was a game-changer. Suddenly, Gary and his crew were performing at premier venues throughout the tri-state area every weekend, earning top dollar while sharing the stage with some of the finest musicians in the industry. Big Al's deep musical connections, paired with Gary's growing influence within The Aristocrats Organization, led to a major milestone: Gary's first opportunity to record a 45 RPM single.

At the time, pressing a single was considered a rite of passage for any serious artist. Backed by The Aristocrats' powerhouse band, the record featured the standout track "Be My Lady," a soulful showcase of soaring lead vocals. The lush harmonies and crisp, tight arrangements showcased the group's collective talent. The B-side, "Don't Go," was a gritty, deep funk cut led by Linda Blakely and featuring a crew of top-tier Louisville musicians. The record was pressed in limited quantity, fewer than 1,000 copies, and quietly became a rare gem among collectors. Years later, interest in the recording was reignited when The Aristocrats appeared on the Sister Funk compilation around the year 2000. That reissue introduced their music to a new generation of soul and funk enthusiasts.

The Aristocrats

Linda Blakely's striking presence in the group commanded attention, especially noted by attendance from male audiences, this feature added a unique layer of versatility and showmanship to their performances. They soon returned to the studio to cut several live tracks, further establishing their sound. But just as their momentum was building, tragedy struck. In the mid-1970s, Albert "Big Al" Workman suffered a sudden heart attack and passed away. His loss was deeply felt not only as a mentor and musical anchor, but as a visionary who had helped shape their path.

In the face of this unexpected loss, the group found solace in their new musical direction shaped through their collaboration with Linda Blakely. Her influence brought a fresh, expressive sound that became the remedy for their grief and allowed them to press forward. Once again, much of the responsibility for keeping the group on course fell on Gary's shoulders. The band continued performing heavily on the nightclub circuit with Linda front and center.
Brad and Linda married, but soon an opportunity came knocking for her as well. Linda was approached with an offer to join the nationally recognized Fatback Band, a move that would take her career to the next level. In the wake of her departure, the group made efforts to regroup and evolve.

Rising from the ashes of their earlier incarnation, they rebranded under a new name: Nature's Own, signaling a fresh chapter built on resilience, talent, and the unshakable foundation they all helped create.

Even in those early days, they vowed to outshine the likes of The O'Jays and The Temptations. Living, believing that perfection was the only standard worth chasing. That wasn't just talk; they believed it with every ounce of their being. To them, perfection wasn't optional; it was the only way to do it right. And the crowd could feel that. Every note hit with intention. Every movement had a purpose. Audiences responded instantly. Women screamed and danced in clubs packed out night after night. On more than one occasion, fire marshals had to shut the doors because the venue was over capacity. It wasn't hype, it was history being made. The group practiced relentlessly, often long after everyone else had gone home. Late into the night, they fine-tuned their harmonies, polished their choreography, and ran their sets over and over until every second landed with power.

If one member missed a beat or a harmony slid slightly out of place, they'd stop cold and start again. No egos, no finger-pointing it wasn't about who was right; it was about what was right. Every practice session was a workout. Voices strained to reach the perfect pitch. Sweat soaked their shirts, all in synch with such delight. Feet choreographed as they drilled routines until muscle memory. They treated the rehearsal room like a sacred space, where excellence was forged and mediocrity had no place.

But beneath all that grit was a deep brotherhood. They pushed one another because they believed in one another. Each member carried the weight of their shared dream: to be more than just a good group, to become legends. Sometimes the pay was barely enough to cover the drive. But it didn't matter.

The crowds kept growing, and with every set, they felt the momentum building. One night stood out more than the rest. It was a modest club on the outskirts of Indianapolis nothing fancy, just a small stage, a good sound system, and an audience that didn't know what was about to hit them. When the band struck the first note, something shifted. The room got still. Silent. Then, a beat later, it exploded. People danced like they'd been waiting their whole lives for that exact sound. There was a charge in the air, something electric, something real. After the set, a local promoter walked straight up to them, handed Gary his card, and said, "You boys got something."

That moment was more than validation; it was confirmation. They weren't chasing dreams anymore. They were living them. Every hour in a hot garage, every late-night rehearsal, every missed party, and worn-out pair of shoes, it was all beginning to pay off. The road ahead was still long. Bigger cities. Bigger stages. But now, they had traction. Momentum.

And even as they packed up after those early gigs, sweaty and exhausted, their minds were already on the next show, how to make it tighter, cleaner, more powerful. How to turn that first spark into a flame no one could ignore. They weren't legends yet. But they were no longer just hopefuls either. They were the business on everybody mind.

Natures Own

Now performing under the banner of Nature's Own, the group remained firmly in their creative groove, still sharp, still hungry, and again, quickly became one of the most popular acts in the Louisville club circuit. Their signature "Ladies' Night" shows were legendary: standing-room-only crowds, women swooning and screaming. Packed houses demanded encores night after night.

Gary's commanding stage presence, paired with his eye for tailored suits and razor-sharp style, made him a natural frontman, cool, composed, and always in control. But it wasn't just about him. All of the group's members were undeniable standouts like Brad, a magnetic performer with unmatched flair. Onstage, Brad transformed. People said he turned into something like a god under the lights, with slick choreography, a piercing falsetto, and an effortless cool that drove the women wild.

As the three friends, Gary, Robert, and Brad, continued to rise, so did their connection. The bond between them deepened. What began as a shared love for music in the neighborhood had evolved into a brotherhood built on trust, hustle, and a shared mission. They weren't just kids chasing a dream anymore; they were artists with purpose, determined to carve out their place in music history.

Their reputation soared on the strength of their "Ladies' Night" show's signature events that weren't just performances but experiences. Word spread fast: if you were looking for velvet-smooth harmonies, a great show, and songs that made you feel something, this was the place to be. Week after week, they sold out venues across Louisville. Women dressed to the nines, men came through in their cleanest fits, and the room would light up the moment the first harmony hit. They didn't just sing, they performed. And the crowd adored them for it. The group had become local celebrities. In the streets, people began to recognize them at the gas station, the barbershop, or the corner store. A nod, a handshake, a "Y'all killed it last week." But what the public didn't always see was what happened behind the scenes.

Behind every performance was tireless work. This wasn't something they just pulled out of thin air; it was built, layer by layer, sweat and patience baked into every note. Most days, they were juggling multiple hustles. After spending the morning detailing cars and handling business, they'd head straight to practice. That old garage became a sacred space, a kind of makeshift studio and rehearsal hall all in one. Dust on the shelves, tools hanging on the walls, and black glass mirrors leaned up against the wall so they could lock in choreography between runs.

They'd run through intricate vocal arrangements over and over. Someone would catch a flat note, and they'd stop everything, rewind, and do it again until it was perfect. Every harmony had to hit just right. Every transition, every pause, every breath was considered. They weren't just standing around; they were moving, tightening their stage presence, making sure their steps matched their sound. In that mirror, they weren't just practicing, they were becoming better entertainers, better Professionals and Better Craftsmen.

The kind of group that didn't just sound good in the moment but left something behind when the show was over. And it wasn't always easy. Sometimes there were arguments, long nights, aching backs, and hoarse voices. But they kept going. Because they believed in the music and in each other, this was more than a group; it was a brotherhood forged through effort, unity, and shared ambition. Each and every night they stepped on stage, the audience saw the shine, but behind that shine was a grind most never knew.

The Shop and the Music

After years of singing under the proverbial streetlights, Gary realized he needed more than these gigs and well-groomed talent to keep his musical dreams alive. He needed to step up his business portfolio. That's when he found a new location for the Shop, and the New G&G Auto Cleaners was born. It was a great spot with three bays and an office space in the Frankfort Avenue area, quickly earning a solid reputation for meticulous, high-quality work. Gary made G&G a profitable cash business and it also became the lifeline of their musical ambitions. After hours, the garage transformed into a rehearsal space where the scent of car wax mixed with the sound of harmonies. Group members, friends, and family worked at the Shop. This was the rehearsal spot between gigs, detailing cars by day, perfecting vocal runs, and choreography by night. The garage was where new arrangements were tested, old favorites were refined, and future show sets came to life.

The income from the Shop kept things flowing, covering travel expenses, wardrobe costs, and studio time. As business boomed, it proved that Gary's relocation effort was a great idea, as it quickly became a go-to place in the city for specialty detailing services. G&G became known not only for its precision cleanup work but also for the high-profile clientele it attracted, including names like NBA Player Derek Smith, who became a regular customer.
The singer, Johnny Paycheck of "Take This Job and Shove It!" fame, came by and dropped off a signed autograph album.
The auto dealer giants at the time, Brown Brothers Cadillac, Bob Ryan "The Smiling Irishman," and Sam Swope of the Swope Auto Group enjoyed their patronage and helped elevate G&G's reputation.

Word of mouth traveled fast. One week, it might be a local radio DJ getting a deep clean before a car show; the next, a touring musician swinging through Louisville for a performance. Gary treated every car like a Cadillac, whether a Ford Escort or a Bentley. His attention to detail and friendly demeanor earned him loyal customers and valuable connections.
Many of these relationships helped build bridges to his music ventures, whether through sponsorships, gigs, or unexpected collaborations.

Meeting and Working with Bobby Lester

Gary had an acquaintance who introduced him to the Louisville singing legend Bobby Lester, who was a founding member and lead singer of The Moonglows. Known for hits like "Sincerely" and "The Ten Commandments of Love," Bobby quickly became a mentor and friend. Bobby owned a Record store in Big A Shopping Center called "Stick it in Your Ear." From that meeting at the Oak Lounge, Gary was introduced to Bobby Lester and sparked the beginning of a resurgence of the pioneering Doo-Wop Group, The Moonglows.

The two men connected over music, and a shared vision for preserving Black vocal harmony traditions. Gary convinced Bobby to get back in the music game with his two partners, Rob and Brad.

Together, they revived Bobby Lester's Career and set in play his new Moonglows. Now, Gary was learning the art of "Bass-Baritone" in Moonglow's Style. A four-part harmony with direction from Bobby Lester himself. Together they began tours on the East Coast, performing to sold-out crowds and earning standing ovations wherever they played. Bobby took the group to New York. They performed a string of live shows, including memorable appearances at iconic venues like Madison Square Gardens and The Beacon Theatre.

They were waiting on a promised call from a recording agent Bobby had been in talks with; this hopeful hustle lasted six months. All of them had bills at home, and it wasn't feeling right being out of town, scraping by, even though they knew they were trying to get established and it would take some time. But how long could they last?

JOEL WHITBURN'S

Record Research

TOP RECORDS

Facts about 4000 Recordings Listed in Billboard's "Best Selling Singles" Charts.

Bobby Lester

AND THE

MOONGLOWS

Bobby Lester (the original lead-singer of of their hits) helped to originate the MOONGLOWS during the very early 50's. and has always been admired for his ability to execute live on stage that same qualitative sound he performed on records. The Moonglows today consist of a self-contained unit fully equipped for shows and/or dance sets in clubs, lounges, concerts etc. yet still featuring the golden sound of BOBBY LESTER. BOBBY LESTER & THE MOONGLOWS is truly a blast out of the past and very much a unique part of the roots of ROCK'N' ROLL.

DATE	POS.	WKS	MOONGLOWS RECORDINGS	
1/24/54	2	20	SINCERELY........................	Chess 1581
4/6/55	11	7	MOST OF ALL	Chess 1589
8/22/56	28	14	SEE SAW	Chess 1629
6/29/57	73	6	PLEASE SEND ME SOMEONE TO LOVE.	Chess 1661
9/21/58	22	16	TEN COMMANDMENTS OF LOVE........	Chess 1705

The Moonglows

This period not only solidified Gary's identity as a dedicated musician and relentless hustler. This time also fostered a sense of unity among the group, a brotherhood bonded by hustle, harmonies, and horsepower. Eventually, things got slow, and after months passed. Brad and Robert became homesick and decided to head back to Louisville. Gary knew his chance was near, but the timing just wasn't right. I guess everything was too much to risk; that's all I can think of. Bobby expressed to Gary, "Life is all about decisions." "Some are Good, Some Are Bad, but they have to be made". Gary wasn't comfortable leaving just yet and tried to convince his brothers to stay as he still believed in the opportunity's potential.

Although Gary knew he should stick it out a little longer with Bobby, he ultimately returned home with Rob and Brad. Shortly after their departure, Bobby received the call he had been waiting for and secured a solo studio session with the Record Agent. Though disappointed Gary wasn't there then, Bobby called him later and extended an invitation to work with him on his new label deal with RCA. The call back went as follows, with Bobby Lester saying Hey, Brother, I know you're Ready now. "It's Show Time!" They returned to New York to perform and recorded some live shows.

The Moonglows

Together, they had brought the group back into the concert
spotlight, performing on primary stages and reconnecting with
new radio audiences eager for authentic doo-wop and soul sounds.
Their partnership bridged generations and reclaimed a place for
The Moonglows in the national music conversation.

Bobby Lester's Moonglows were experiencing a powerful
resurgence with Gary Rodgers in the mix, and the group began
drawing large crowds again. Their timeless harmonies and stage
presence showed this comeback wasn't just about nostalgia, it was
a revival that brought The Moonglows' legacy to new generations
and cemented their lasting influence on music.

Solemn Oath to Keep
the Sound Alive

As Gary and Bobby Lester's partnership grew, Gary took on more than just singing duties. He became the group's manager and promoter, handling bookings, publicity, and logistics while running his detailing shop. It was a demanding balance, but Gary thrived in the dual role. Before Bobby passed in 1980, He asked Gary to make him a solemn oath. That was to keep "The Moonglows' Sound" Alive. Honoring that promise, Gary took up the mantle and renamed the group Bobby Lester's Magnificent Moonglows. Gary was determined to make this Moonglows operation a success, and from the demands of this work, not everyone would continue the journey.

There were many Moonglows member replacements throughout the years one was my mom's brother Bruce Martin. There was Gene Kelly, James Pete Crawford, Johnny "Oink" Franklin, Robert Ford, William Bradley McPhatter son of (Clyde McPhatter), Norman Curd (guitarist and music director) was a good friend of my Dad for many years. There were numerous other members. Gary kept his word, went to work branding and promoting the Magnificent Moonglows brand. As a rule number one, Gary always looked into setting up negotiating better-paying gigs, securing radio interviews and television spots also organizing concert appearances from Louisville to the East Coast

Under Gary's direction, this Moonglows group mastered tight four-part harmonies and polished their stage routines, giving audiences a show that honored the Moonglows' original sound while adding fresh energy.

Bobby Lester's Magnificent Moonglows

For Gary, this wasn't just about keeping a name alive; it was about honoring a musical lineage, preserving a sound that shaped a generation, and carving out space for it in a changing world. But the road ahead wasn't smooth. As Gary poured his heart into building the group's presence and sharpening their performances, the pressure of constant travel, late-night rehearsals, and the high standards he set took a toll.

Robert Ford was killed by a hit-and-run driver. That was devastating to everyone. Our world was crushed because Robert was Brad and my Dad's brother. Over the years, members came and went, some drawn by the allure of the stage, others bowing out when the grind became too much. Despite the rotating cast, Gary remained the constant, the compass and heartbeat of the operation. Among those who stepped in along the way were people who left their mark on the group's evolving story. Many thanks to everyone for helping, especially Norman Curd. He was a gifted guitarist who served as the Music Director and a close friend. Norman helped shape the group's musical arrangements, ensuring their sound was both respectful of tradition and engaging for modern audiences.

Magnificent Moonglows

Yes, there were many others who didn't get named, but for a season or a stretch, added their voices and talents to the legacy. Each contributed a piece to the ever-growing story of the Magnificent Moonglows. Though faces changed, the mission remained the same: honor the past, electrify the present, and inspire the future. Gary continued to work, tireless in his pursuit of growth. He became not just the group's lead singer but its manager, publicist, booking agent, and creative director. He hustled hard, negotiating gigs, locking in radio interviews, and ensuring that the Moonglows' name appeared on marquee signs up and down the East Coast. From local spots in Louisville to prestigious stages in cities like Washington, D.C., Philadelphia, and New York. The Magnificent Moonglows began to build a new reputation, one rooted in history, but forged through relentless drive.

Under Gary's leadership, the group perfected their craft. They locked in their four-part harmonies with surgical precision, rehearsing for hours to ensure every blend and vocal transition hit with emotion and power. Their choreography was tight, their wardrobes sharp, and their performances heartfelt. Every show felt like a revival, an invitation to remember the past while witnessing something vibrant and alive. Audiences responded. People who had grown up with the original Moonglows found themselves swept up in nostalgia, while younger listeners were introduced to a genre they'd only heard secondhand.

Always, at the center, was Gary holding it all together, honoring Bobby Lester's memory with every step he took, every note he sang, and every stage he commanded. What Gary was building wasn't just a tribute group or a musical act. He was building a legacy of his own, carefully stitched into the larger story of one of doo-wop's most iconic names.

The Magnificent Moonglows were living proof that a great sound never dies, it just finds new voices to carry it forward. And Gary, ever faithful to his promise, made sure those voices were ready.

Magnificent Moonglows

Int. Cl.: 41

Prior U.S. Cl.: 107

United States Patent and Trademark Office Reg. No. 1,248,675
Registered Aug. 16, 1983

SERVICE MARK
Principal Register

MAGNIFICENT MOONGLOWS

B. L. Production Inc. (Kentucky corporation)
3621 Regataway
Louisville, Ky. 40211

For ENTERTAINMENT SERVICES RENDERED BY A VOCAL AND INSTRUMENTAL GROUP, in CLASS 41 (U.S. Cl. 107).
First use Sep. 1951; in commerce Sep. 1951.

Ser. No. 366,218. filed May 24, 1982.

MARY L. SPARROW, Examining Attorney

Gary remained deeply connected to Bobby Lester's family after his passing, not just as a musical partner but as someone who genuinely cared. He stayed close to Mom Bert, Bobby's mother, offering steady support and companionship during these difficult times of losing Bobby. Gary was also a mentor to Bobby's son Stephon "Newt." Dallas. When record company executives came to visit Mom Bert, she called Gary and had him step into a larger role, assisting with the management and preservation of Bobby Lester's estate. Ultimately, Gary became the guardian of the Moonglows' legacy, both in name and in practice.

True to the promise he had made, Gary rebranded the group Bobby Lester's Magnificent Moonglows, a gesture that ensured Bobby's contributions would never be forgotten. But this wasn't just a name change it was a mission. Gary took the responsibility seriously. He became the driving force behind every decision, working tirelessly to elevate the group's presence, preserve its sound, and introduce its magic to new generations. The work wasn't easy. Building and maintaining the group became a constant process of trial and error. Gary knew the importance of getting the harmonies just right. If the blend was off even slightly —he wasn't afraid to make changes. Over the years, there were many new faces—some stayed for a season, others longer.

Magnificent Moonglows

But each change was made with one goal in mind: keeping the spirit and sound of the original Moonglows alive and strong.

The lifestyle that followed was demanding. Life on the road became the norm, long drives, late nights, technical riders, and endless soundchecks. They played venues big and small, from local clubs in Louisville to theaters up and down the East Coast. Gary wore many hats: lead singer, manager, booking agent, promoter. And despite the hustle, he never let the quality slip. Every night was a chance to win over a new crowd, to remind people why this music mattered. And no matter where the road led, they always circled back to their home base: the Shop.

More than just Gary's workplace, it doubled as the group's headquarters. It was where they rehearsed, handled business, and gathered to plan their next moves. Buffing stations, vacuum cleaners, and supplies with a washer and dryer shared space with microphones and music stands. It was a humble space, but it had heart and it was theirs. After weekends on the road, the guys would regroup there to work on arrangements, take calls from promoters, review contracts, and reconnect as a unit.

For Gary, it wasn't just about the music; it was about the brotherhood they built around it. He was balancing the demands of the group with family life, running the shop, and keeping the Moonglows' legacy intact. Through all the changes, he stayed true to the promise he made to Bobby Lester. He wasn't just keeping the Moonglows alive; he was giving them new life in every way, whether on stage or in large venues, the harmony continued. On that right-hand side was always Gary, steady, committed, and endlessly driven, who made sure that harmony had a home.

Magnificent Moonglows

B. L. PRODUCTIONS, Inc.

AGREEMENT made this _______________________ day of _____________________ , 19 _________ ,

between ____ (hereinafter

referred to as "ARTIST") and ____
(hereinafter referred to as "PURCHASER").

It is mutually agreed between the parties as follows:

The PURCHASER hereby engages the ARTIST and the ARTIST hereby agrees to perform the engagement hereinafter provided, upon all of the terms and conditions herein set forth, including those hereof entitled "Additional Terms and Condition."

1. PLACE OF ENGAGEMENT ____

    Exact address ____

2. DATE(s) OF ENGAGEMENT ____

3. HOURS OF ENGAGEMENT ____

4. REHEARSAL(s) ____

5. FULL PRICE AGREED UPON ____

All payments shall be paid by certified check, money order, bank draft or cash as follows:

    (a) $ _________________ shall be paid by PURCHASER to and in the name of ARTIST'S agent,

        B. L. Productions, Inc., not later than ____ ;

    (b) $ _________________ shall be paid by PURCHASER to ARTIST not later than ________________

6. SPECIAL PROVISIONS ____
____
____
____

(ARTIST) _______________________________________

By ____

All signed copies must be returned
to B. L. Productions, Inc. by

(PURCHASER) ___________________________________

By ____

Address: _______________________________________

Phone: ____

THE ABOVE SIGNATURES CONFIRM THAT THE PARTIES HAVE READ AND APPROVED THIS AGREEMENT.

Magnificent Moonglows

While on the East Coast, they headlined shows, packed theaters, ballrooms, and Doo- Wop revivals. They were reconnecting The Moonglows with old fans and winning over new ones. Gary said their most loyal homes away from home were in Pittsburgh, The United Group Harmony Association. "Ronnie I" Italiano was the founder of the UGHA. The local audiences loved Bobby Lester's Moonglows. The city of Pittsburgh embraced them as family. Year after year, they returned to sold-out shows and standing ovations. Namely, the UGHA became one of their favorite concert events. Rest In Peace, Ronnie I. God bless the Family, and thank you all.

Bobby Lester's Magnificent Moonglows didn't just bring Doo-Wop back to community halls and theaters; they returned to the national spotlight, thanks in no small part to Gary's relentless drive and sharp vision. Under his leadership, the group earned opportunities that many thought were long gone for a classic vocal act from a bygone era. Gary didn't just chase nostalgia; he positioned the Moonglows as relevant, in-demand performers who could bring their timeless harmony to any stage, for any audience.

Magnificent Moonglows

One of the most unforgettable milestones came with a private performance at a birthday celebration for actress Brooke Shields. The invitation itself was a testament to how far Gary had elevated the group's reputation. In an event, New York Celebrities were the backdrop. The Moonglows brought their signature sound to an elite gathering, reminding even the most high-profile guests of the enduring magic of true harmony.

Their presence at such a star-studded event proved that the Moonglows weren't just a cherished memory, they were a living, breathing act capable of captivating audiences across generations. Another standout engagement came at the iconic Playboy Club in Lansing, Michigan. A venue that had long hosted some of the biggest names in entertainment. For Gary and the group, this wasn't just a show it was a statement.

Performing on that stage meant they had earned their way into the upper tier of American live music venues. The show was electric. The crowd was on their feet, drawn in by the polished vocals, sharp choreography, comedy skits, and undeniable presence that had become the group's hallmark under Gary's guidance. The energy in the room wasn't just about performance it was about revival, recognition, and respect.

Magnificent Moonglows

Gary's leadership did more than revive a name; it reestablished Bobby Lester's Moonglows as a force on the national concert circuit. He understood the importance of brand, presentation, and professionalism, and he worked tirelessly to ensure that every detail from the setlists to the suits reflected the excellence the group was known for. Whether it was a concert hall in Philadelphia, a gala in New York, or a private party in L.A., the Moonglows brought the same precision, passion, and soul to the stage. Gary's vision took them beyond just being a legacy act. He transformed the Moonglows into ambassadors of a genre, bridging the gap between eras, and reminding audiences, young and old, of the deep emotional power of vocal harmony.

Every high-profile performance, every prestigious booking, was a victory not just for Gary and the group, but for the music they were determined to preserve and promote. In every note they sang, there was a tribute to the past. But in every stage they conquered, there was a clear sign: The Moonglows were still very much in the present and going nowhere but forward. Gary reorganized his shop and business continued to pick up. Gary enlisted a longtime friend to run the shop. He seemed to be able to handle the management responsibilities well enough to keep the shop running. He was the back up plan in case they have to leave town on Moonglows' business.

The Moonglows once again were the hottest show on the East Coast. One night at a hotel they were performing at in Pittsburgh a large fire broke out late into the night. Gary made the newspaper as he was hailed a hero for saving an elderly lady who was trapped in a room where flames and smoke were threatening life.

Everyone made it out safely and when he called home left a word
that said "he would be another 3 weeks out on the road as they got
more gigs booked from this one".
There were problems starting at the home front. The manager
stopped checking in with the daily numbers from The Shop.
Gary's life was drawn and quartered by his many responsibilities.

He loved his wife, and his family very much and to top things off
his Detail shop would be run in the ground if left alone any longer.
Countless afternoons were spent perfecting harmonies and
polishing choreography after washing cars, cleaning interiors, and
buffing paint jobs. Gary's leadership revitalized the Moonglows,
ensuring their sound and legacy thrived well into the modern era,
blending hustle, heart, and harmony into every note and every
mile of their journey. His leadership didn't just restore the group's
harmony; it gave it new meaning.

With Gary at the helm, the Moonglows were more than a vocal
group they were a movement. He infused their journey with a
tireless hustle, balancing business savvy with musical excellence.
Under his guidance, every polished note mirrored a gleaming
fender; every tight harmony, a testament to persistence.

The Moonglows evolved without losing their soul. Their music matured, retaining the velvet-smooth charm of its origins while embracing contemporary rhythms and sensibilities. Gary's vision ensured their legacy not only endured but thrived carried forward by each performance, each fan, and every mile traveled in pursuit of perfect harmony. Blending sweat and soul, work and wonder, the Moonglows turned everyday moments into a stage, leaving behind a story as enduring as their sound.

Date	Pos.	Wks.	MOONGLOWS Recordings	Label
11/24/54	2	20	Sincerely	Chess 1581
4/6/55	11	7	Most Of All	Chess 1589
8/22/56	28	14	See Saw	Chess 1629
6/29/57	73	6	Please Send Me Someone To Love	Chess 1661
9/21/58	22	16	Ten Commandments Of Love	Chess 1705

OTHER HITS	Label
We Go Together	Chess
Oh Whistle My Love	Chance
Secret Love	Chance
Sincerely 72	RCA
You've Chosen Me	RCA
Over and Over Again	Chess
(From the movie Rock, Rock, Rock)	

Magnificent Moonglows

Stars of Stage
Radio & T.V.

B. L. PRODUCTIONS INC.
2309 Osage Ave.
Louisville, Ky. 40210

BOBBY LESTER'S
MAGNIFICENT MOONGLOWS
R.C.A. Records

GARY RODGERS
Executive Director
(502) 778-0766

Gary Rodgers loved the music but wasn't content with just singing and running the detailing business. He started Pisces of Louisville Fish Catering, where he quickly gained fortune and a different source of fame with a groundbreaking Secret Recipe. Although he was still entertaining thousands at events, this was just a different type of performance. Some of his most profitable shows were at massive gatherings like the Cincinnati Jazz Festival and the Indiana Black Expo over 30,000 people in attendance.

Thunder Over Louisville and the Screaming Eagles Motorcycle Club's annual event in Louisville was very popular during The Kentucky Derby Weekend in Louisville, KY. Thousands of people packed parks or wherever Pisces was located in the festivals. The people wanted Pisces, and Gary made a fortune by selling his famous fish and sides to hungry crowds. It was rumored Gary's Pisces of Louisville made a Million Dollars in 1989 and by the way the crowds were lined up, no one would doubt it.

Magnificent Moonglows

As the years passed, their bond with the original Moonglows frontman, Harvey Fuqua, only deepened. Rooted not just in shared melodies, but in a profound mutual respect for the legacy they were preserving and evolving together. What began as admiration soon blossomed into a partnership, as Gary and the group seamlessly stepped into a role that honored the past while breathing new life into it.

They didn't simply perform the Moonglows' timeless catalog they lived it, shaped it, and shared it with audiences who may never have heard those harmonies live if not for their efforts.

Gary and the group joined Harvey on several stages across the country, from intimate venues to the nationally televised PBS specials and Doo Wop 50's Celebratory events.

Each Moonglows' performance wasn't just a tribute it was a continuation, a living thread between the golden age of Doo-Wop and the present. Together, they performed the old classics with reverence and flair, weaving the silky harmonies and tight choreography into shows that felt both nostalgic and fresh. Captive audiences, some hearing these songs for the first time, were loving the authenticity and soul that Gary and Harvey brought to every Moonglows' note.

Magnificent Moonglows

Behind the scenes, they traveled side by side, shared long rehearsals, and swapped stories from different generations of the music industry. Harvey Fuqua a legend in his own right and famously meticulous in his pursuit of musical excellence recognized something rare in Gary: an unshakable dedication that mirrored his own. Gary wasn't merely filling shoes; he was helping pave new roads while walking alongside giants. Harvey saw in Gary not just a Moonglows protégé, but a kindred spirit someone who loved the music not for fame or nostalgia, but for its power to move people.

Their relationship became more than professional; it was family. The time they spent together forged a deep friendship built on artistry and a shared mission to keep the Moonglows' spirit alive. With every harmony sung, every crowd moved, and every mile traveled. Gary and the group fulfilled that mission, honoring the legacy Harvey and Bobby built while adding new chapters to its enduring story.

Magnificent Moonglows

Magnificent Moonglows

I remember my dad and I sitting on his couch, his voice was filled with excitement he said "Guess what, Rodge? I got a call from the Rock and Roll Hall of Fame! in Cleveland, Ohio. I said Really? They want me to represent Bobby and The Moonglows' induction into the Rock and Roll Hall of Fame. I have to get in touch with Harvey, Prentiss, and Pete to get set up for a performance." We were ecstatic. For my Dad, this honor was deeply meaningful but also bittersweet. This moment was one of triumph, yet it echoed silently with the absence of Bobby Lester, the Moonglows' original lead singer, mentor, and the man who had shaped so much of Gary's musical journey.
Bobby had passed away years earlier, but his voice, wisdom, and presence remained etched in Gary's heart.

Magnificent Moonglows

Now, Gary was prepared to accept the award on Bobby's behalf, carrying not only the name but also the spirit of a man who had taught him more than just how to sing. He taught him about discipline, showmanship, business acumen, and above all, loyalty and friendship. It was a moment Gary had long prepared for, even if he hadn't known it. And true to his nature, a man of action and heart, he wasted no time. My dad picked up the phone and called Harvey. Without hesitation, Harvey said "Yes!" The Moonglows would reunite once again, not just to perform, but to celebrate a lifetime of music and to honor the legacy that had brought them all together.

Within days, plans were in motion. Flights were booked, hotel rooms reserved, and rehearsals went on with a precision that spoke to their experience and passion. Gary made sure every detail was accounted for, he knew this night was bigger than any one of them. It was about preserving a legacy, recognizing the pioneers who paved the way, and showing the world that the spirit of Doo Wop, harmony, and brotherhood was still alive.

In a matter of days, the Moonglows were ready. Voices warmed, suits pressed, shoes shined. They rehearsed, set to step onto one of music's biggest stages in New York, not only as performers, but as torchbearers of an era that still had stories to tell. For Gary, it wasn't just about recognition. It was about responsibility, about carrying forward a legacy entrusted to him by Bobby, affirmed by Harvey, and sustained by every note they had ever sung together.

Magnificent Moonglows

The air inside New York City's Waldorf Astoria shimmered with the electricity of music history in the making. The Moonglows, one of the most influential Doo-Wop groups of the 1950s, were about to receive long-awaited recognition. On that unforgettable night in the year 2000, the ballroom was lined wall to wall with legends among the biggest names in this class were Bonnie Raitt, Earth Wind and Fire, and producer Clive Davis, just to name drop.

Gary Rodgers stood among them, as always dressed sharp, this time black tuxedo, his familiar warm smile both proud and humbled. It had been a fun road from the city of Louisville, singing and commanding stages from Atlantic City to Phoenix. The Moonglows finally received recognition and acknowledgment of their rightful place among the greats in the Rock & Roll Hall of Fame. Paul Simon, the legendary singer-songwriter, took the stage to introduce "The Moonglows." Gary felt a rush of memories as the induction speech honored their contribution to Doo-Wop harmony and its golden era.

He remembered Bobby's confident stance at the microphone, heard the tight four-part harmonies in his mind, and felt the weight of the years of late nights, narrow highways, small-town clubs, and packed theaters. When their names were called, Gary and his fellow members took the stage to perform.

Magnificent Moonglows

Their harmonies soared, seasoned voices blending, not quite like they were in their youth, but reminding everyone present why The Moonglows had been, and would always be, something special. The applause, gracious as thunderous, was seen as a wave of appreciation long overdue. After the performance, the group remained onstage as they were presented with their Hall of Fame awards.

Holding the trophy in his hand, Gary spoke from the heart. He thanked the fans, his family, the city of Louisville, and, most of all, Bobby Lester. "Without Bobby, I wouldn't be standing here tonight," he said, his voice thick with emotion. "He sang about love, life and that music still lives today." It was a night that immortalized the legacy of a group and, for Gary Rodgers, validated a lifetime of dedication to the music he loved.

Magnificent Moonglows

Gary Rodgers' legacy is preserved across generations of media. His musical work has been chronicled in the pages of JET, EBONY, The Source and Rolling Stone magazines. He has also appeared in newspapers, television specials, and through recordings on CDs, cassette tapes, DVDs, and countless other formats. Each one a testament to his years of relentless dedication to music. His body of work stands as a lasting proof of a man who approached every endeavor with precision. Gary Rodgers gave his life, style, class, and the highest level of showmanship all in service of preserving and honoring The Moonglows' legacy.

His story lives on, not just in awards and archives but in the voices of those who sing and listen to Moonglows' songs today. Gary's memory continues to live forever in the entrepreneurial spirit carried forward by his family and those who knew him.

Magnificent Moonglows

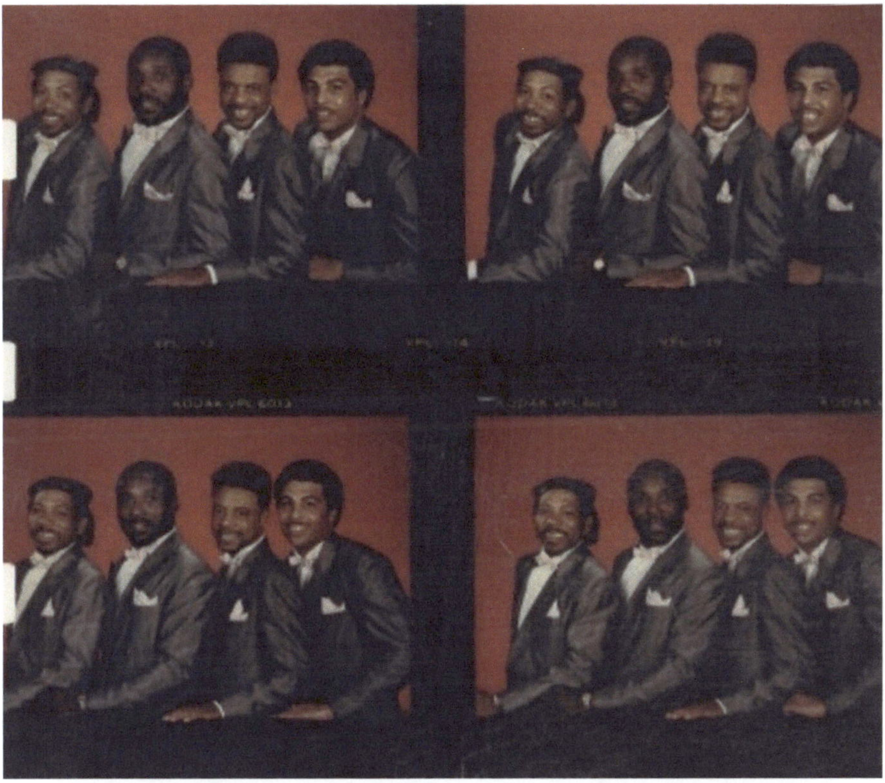

Stars of Stage
Radio & T.V.

B. L. PRODUCTIONS INC.
3621 Regatta Way
Louisville, Ky. 40211

BOBBY LESTER'S
MAGNIFICENT MOONGLOWS
R.C.A. Records

GARY RODGERS
Executive Director
(502) 897-9618

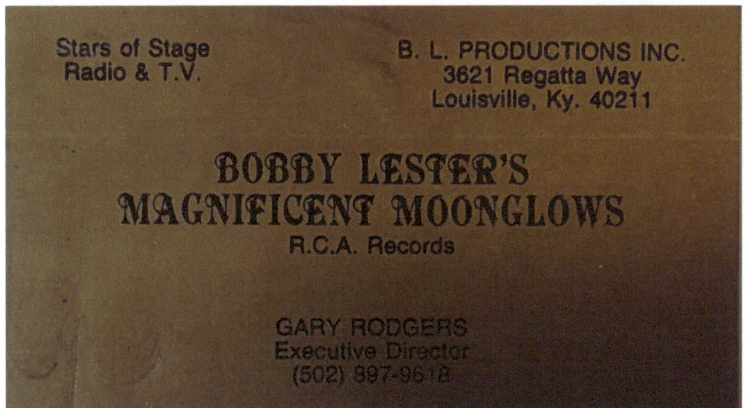

Magnificent Moonglows

Magnificent Moonglows

Magnificent Moonglows

Magnificent Moonglows

A Legacy Remembered

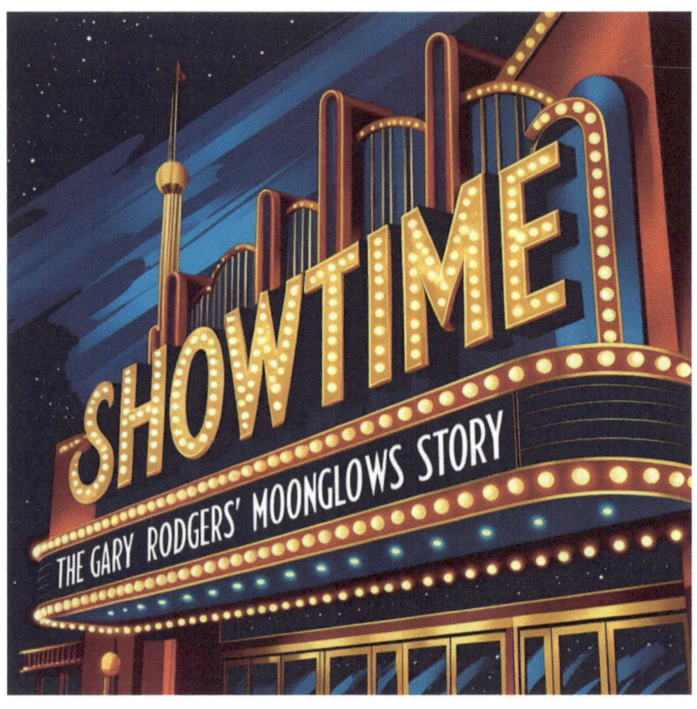

Show Time The Gary Rodgers' Moonglows Story
Written by Gary T. Rodgers Jr. © 2025
Photographs Courtesy of: Private Collections, Anonymous and or
Unknown Sources. Special thanks to the families, fans, and
historians who helped preserve the story.
This Book is dedicated to the voices and those behind the scenes
that shaped a generation. And to everyone that in some way
helped keep the Moonglows Sound Alive.

ShowTime

The Gary Rodgers' Moonglows Story: It is a powerful journey through the life of Gary Rodgers a Louisville Original who completed his musical mission. Honoring a Solemn Oath to his Dear Friend Bobby Lester by preserving and moving forward the legacy of one of R&B's most legendary groups, The Moonglows. With grit, soul, and a deep respect for the music, Gary kept the group's spirit alive long after the spotlight faded, touring, recording, and carrying the name with pride. ShowTime is about going hard everyday, making no excuses and staying true when the world moves on.
Told in a bold, spoken-word
style, this is the untold story of Gary Rodgers and the Moonglows
sound he refused to let die.
More than a music story.

Erika The Billionaire Publishing